Collins

EXPLORE ENGLISH

Student's Coursebook 1

William Collins' dream of knowledge for all began with the publication of his first book in 1819.

A self-educated mill worker, he not only enriched millions of lives, but also founded a flourishing publishing house. Today, staying true to this spirit, Collins books are packed with inspiration, innovation and practical expertise. They place you at the centre of a world of possibility and give you exactly what you need to explore it.

Collins. Freedom to teach.

An imprint of HarperCollins*Publishers*
The News Building
1 London Bridge Street
London SE1 9GF

HarperCollins*Publishers*
Macken House, 39/40 Mayor Street Upper, Dublin 1,
DO1 C9W8,
Ireland

Browse the complete Collins catalogue at
www.collins.co.uk

British Library Cataloguing in Publication Data

A catalogue record for this publication is available from the British Library.

Author and series editor: Daphne Paizee
Publisher: Elaine Higgleton
Product Manager: Lucy Cooper
Development Editor: Cait Hawkins
Project Manager: Lucy Hobbs
Proof reader: Sonya Newland
Cover design: Gordon MacGilp
Cover artwork: Reprinted by permission of HarperCollins Publishers Ltd © 2016 (James Carter)
Internal design: Ken Vail Graphic Design
Typesetter: QBS Learning
Illustrations: QBS Learning and Beehive Illustrations
Production controller: Lyndsey Rogers

Printed and bound in the UK by Martins the Printers

This book contains FSC™ certified paper and other controlled sources to ensure responsible forest management.

For more information visit: www.harpercollins.co.uk/green

Text acknowledgements

The publishers gratefully acknowledge the permissions granted to reproduce copyright material in the book. Every effort has been made to contact the holders of copyright material, but if any have been inadvertently overlooked, the Publisher will be pleased to make the necessary arrangements at the first opportunity.

p88 poem 'The Ball Song' by Tony Mitton from *Playtime Rhymes*, compiled by John Foster published by Oxford University Press 1998, reprinted by permission of David Higham Associates.

HarperCollins*Publishers* Limited for: Artwork from *My Family Tree* by Zoe Clarke, illustrated by Anne Wilson, text © 2010 Zoe Clarke. Artwork from *Bad Bat* by Laura Hambleton, illustrated by Laura Hambleton, text © 2011 Laura Hambleton. Artwork from *What's for Breakfast?* by Paul Shipton, illustrated by Jon Stuart, text © 2006 Paul Shipton. Artwork from *Bob's Secret Hideaway* by Tom Dickinson, illustrated by Jimothy Oliver, text © 2014 Tom Dickinson. Artwork from Jack and the Beanstalk by Caryl Hart, illustrated by Nicola L. Robinson, text © 2013 Caryl Hart. Artwork from *The Oak Tree* by Anna Owen, illustrated by Laszlo Veres, text © 2005 Anna Owen. Artwork from *Bones* by Jonathan Emmett and Alan Baker, artwork by Steve Lumb, text © 2010 Jonathan Emmett and Alan Baker. Artwork from *Sam the Big, Bad Cat* by Sheila Bird, illustrated by Trish Phillips, text © 2005 Sheila Bird. Artwork from *A Day Out* by Anna Owen, illustrated by Andy Hammond, text © 2005 Anna Owen.

Photo acknowledgements

The publishers wish to thank the following for permission to reproduce photographs. Every effort has been made to trace copyright holders and to obtain their permission for the use of copyright materials. The publishers will gladly receive any information enabling them to rectify any error or omission at the first opportunity.

(t = top, c = centre, b = bottom, r = right, l = left)

P61t Kencana Studio/Shutterstock, p61c Omer N Raja/Shutterstock, p61b Solphoto/Shutterstock, p72a Corepics VOF/Shutterstock, p72b stephen rudolph/Shutterstock, p72d Syda Productions/Shutterstock p72e Stefan Holm/Shutterstock, p72f Margo Harrison/Shutterstock, p72g Maciej Kopaniecki/Shutterstock, p72h shinobi/Shutterstock, p72i Bplanet/Shutterstock, p72j 9comeback/Shutterstock, p81f 9comeback/Shutterstock, p82h Ruslan Kudrin/Shutterstock, p82i Karina Bakalyan/Shutterstock, p82j Roman Sigaev/Shutterstock, p101l Skreidzeleu/Shutterstock, p101r Alamy/dbimages, p105l Getty Images/Digital Vision/Lottie Davies, p105c Skreidzeleu/Shutterstock, p105r Alamy/Andy Hockridge, p115a f9photos/Shutterstock, p115b Eky Studio/Shutterstock, p115c TravelMediaProductions/Shutterstock, p115d Bon Appetit/Shutterstock, p119tr ghrzuzudu/Shutterstock, p119br Sergey Uryadnikov/Shutterstock

With thanks to the following teachers and schools for reviewing materials in development: Hawar International School; Melissa Brobst, International School of Budapest; Niki Tzorzis, Pascal Primary School Lemessos.

Contents

Unit 1 Our school

Week 1 What's your name?

1 **Colour in all the letters in your name.**

Write your name.

_____

2 Draw a picture of yourself. Write your name.

My name is _____.

My name begins with _____.

3 **Draw a picture of your friend. Trace and complete the sentence.**

This is _____.

Week 2 In my classroom

1 Listen and write the first letter of each word.

computer	eraser	scissors
crayon	pencil	table
door	ruler	whiteboard

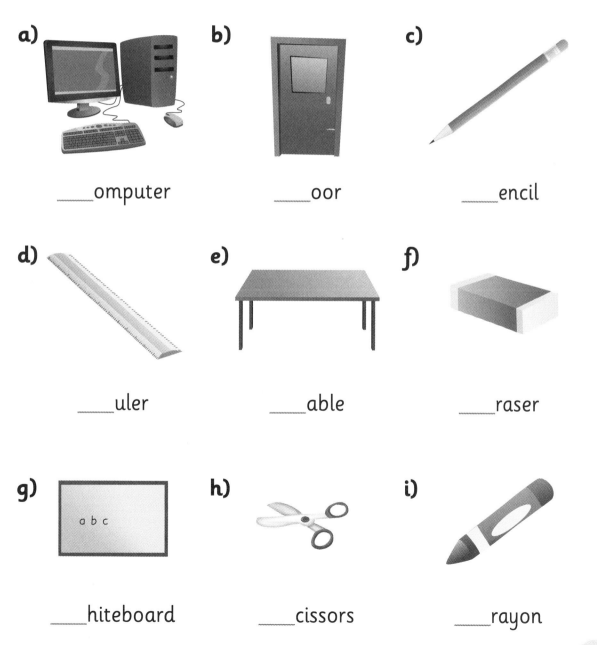

a) _____omputer

b) _____oor

c) _____encil

d) _____uler

e) _____able

f) _____raser

g) _____hiteboard

h) _____cissors

i) _____rayon

2 Choose the correct word. Write the word under the picture.

bin	pen	book	bag

a)

_____

b)

_____

c)

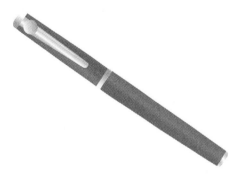

_____

d)

_____

3 **What letter does each word begin with?**
Circle the correct letter.

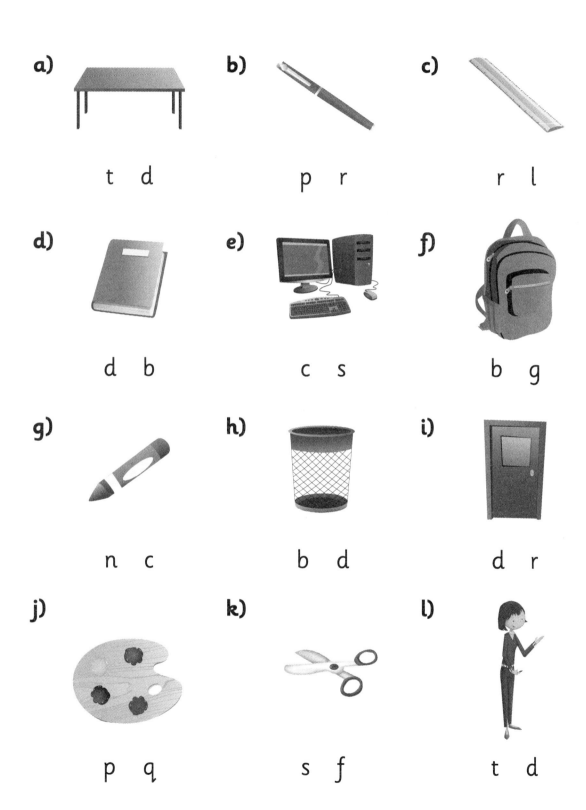

a)
t   d

b)
p   r

c)
r   l

d)
d   b

e)
c   s

f)
b   g

g)
n   c

h)
b   d

i)
d   r

j)
p   q

k)
s   f

l)
t   d

4 Listen and circle. One has been done for you.

a bag   crayons   scissors   a table   a pencil

5 Trace the words. Say each word.

pen

pens

book

books

ruler

rulers

6 Write *his* or *her* under each picture. The first one has been done for you.

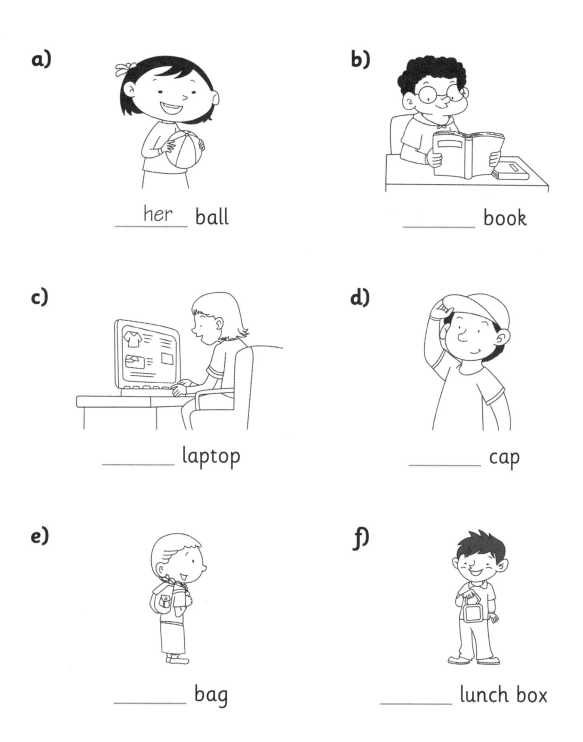

a)

___her___ ball

b)

_____ book

c)

_____ laptop

d)

_____ cap

e)

_____ bag

f)

_____ lunch box

7 **Which path has the letters of the alphabet in the correct order? Where does this path take the girl?**

Week 3 What I do at school

1 **Listen and match the words and the pictures.**
   The first one has been done for you.

a) run

b) read

c) skip

d) listen

e) jump

f) sing

g) write

h) play

2 Now copy the words under the pictures.

3 Listen and tick ✓ the pictures.

Open your book.

Sit down.

Catch the ball.

Come inside.

Paint a picture.

Stand up and sing.

4 **Complete the picture of the classroom. Show what is in your classroom. Talk about your picture.**

Unit 1 Progress check

1 Listen and tick ✓ the pictures.

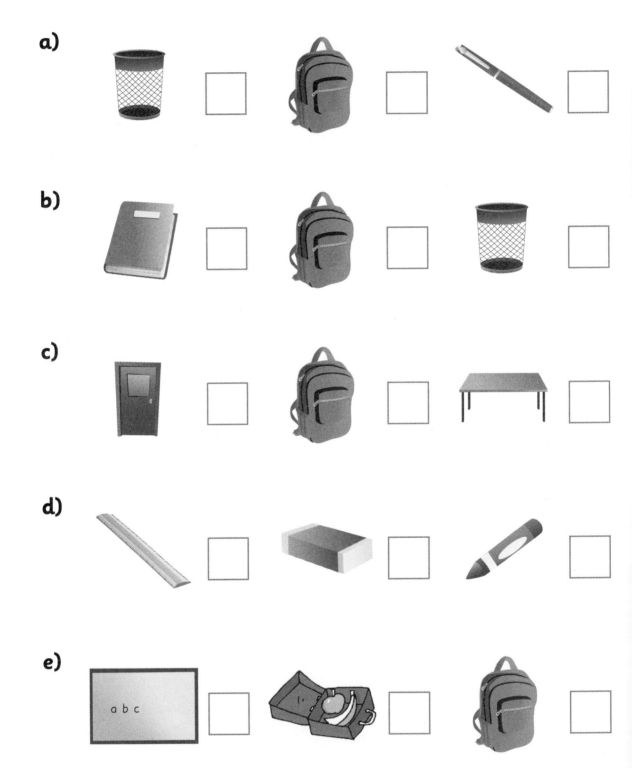

a)

b)

c)

d)

e)

2 Listen and write the first letter.

a)

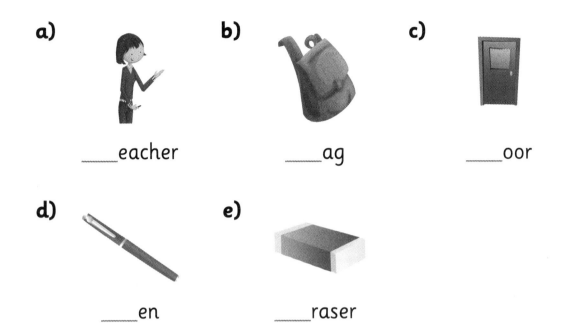

_____eacher

b)

_____ag

c)

_____oor

d)

_____en

e)

_____raser

3 Circle the two words that are the same in each box. One has been done for you.

(his)	her	(his)	is
her	his	her	him
pen	pen	peg	men
bag	bin	bag	bed
name	game	no	name
is	in	is	it

Unit 2 All about me

Week 1 All about me!

1 **Circle the two words that are the same in each box. One has been done for you.**

Ⓘ	you	eye	Ⓘ

you	yes	you	he

he	she	he	her

she	see	she	sea

it	in	it	to

we	will	we	when

they	this	they	that

2 Tick ✓ the correct word.

a)

he ☐

she ☐

b)

they ☐

it ☐

c)

she ☐

it ☐

d)

I ☐

they ☐

3 **Complete the capital letters of the alphabet.**

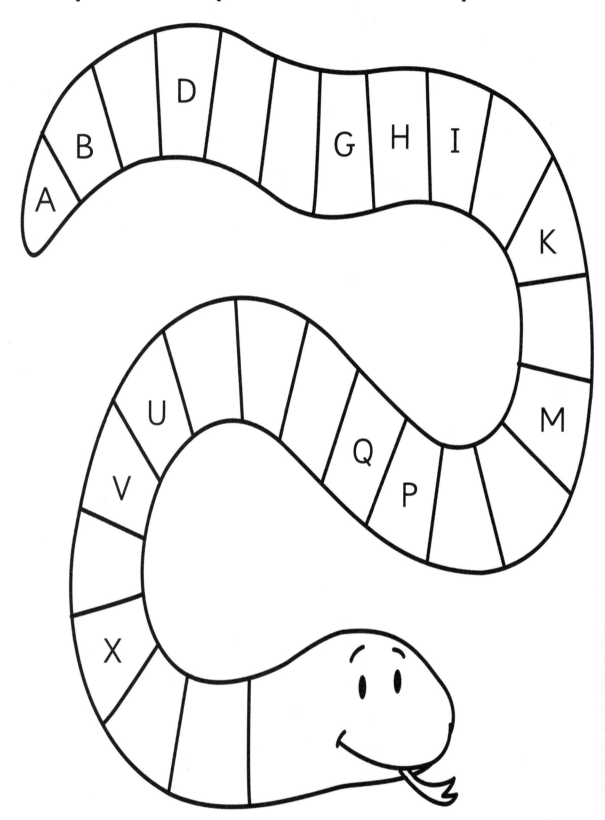

4 **Listen. Complete each of these names with a capital letter from the box.**

V	K	M	A	F	T	S	L	D

a) ____ue

b) ____nton

c) ____oni

d) ____ary

e) ____ernando

f) ____aren

g) ____on

h) ____ihaan

i) ____ucy

Write the names of three friends. Start with capital letters.

_____

_____

_____

5 **Draw a picture of yourself, or glue in a photo.**

6 **Complete the sentences about yourself.**

My name is _____.

I am _____ years old.

I am a _____.

_____ is my friend.

Week 2 My family

1 Circle all the words that begin with *b*.

brother   boy   dog   book

bag   girl   ball

2 Who are these people? Write the first two letters.

_____ _____andma   _____ _____andpa

3 Circle the words that end in *-er*.

Here   are   my   father   and   my   grandmother.

4 Read the story *My Family Tree* in the Student's Resource Book again.

- Complete the family tree.
- Use words from the box.

| brother | dad | grandparents | mum | sister |

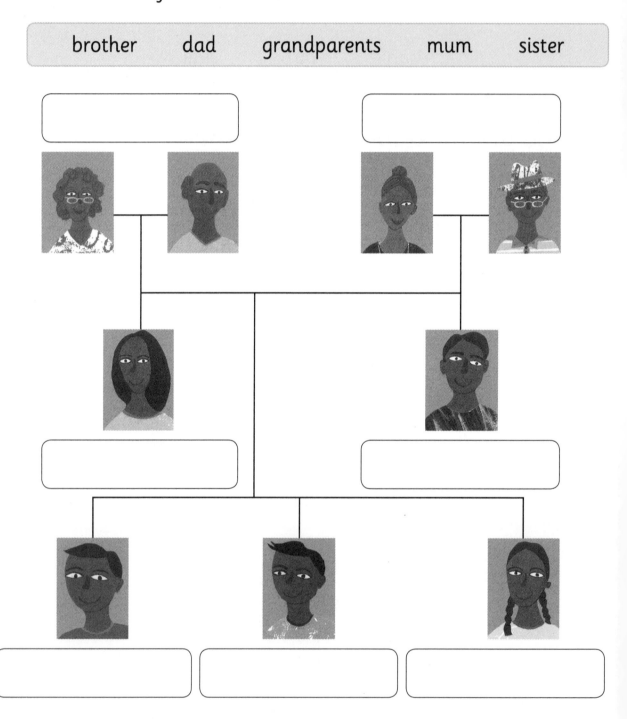

5 **Draw a picture of your family. Label your picture.**

6 Look at the picture of Jo and his family. Listen.

Jo's family

Nina Sara Lizzie Max Jo

7 Answer the questions.

a) Who is in Jo's family? Write their names.

_____Jo_____ _____ _____ _____ _____

b) How old is Jo? _____

c) How old is the baby? _____

d) Jo's mum is called _____.

8 **Listen to the words. Circle the first letter in each word. Say the sounds. The first one has been done for you.**

a) (f)ather

b) sister

c) brother

d) mother

e) grandma

f) dad

9 **Listen to the words. Circle the middle letter in each word. Say the sounds. The first one has been done for you.**

a) m(u)m

b) dad

c) dog

d) bag

e) pen

f) bin

g) bed

h) run

Week 3 What I do at home

1 Match the words and the pictures.

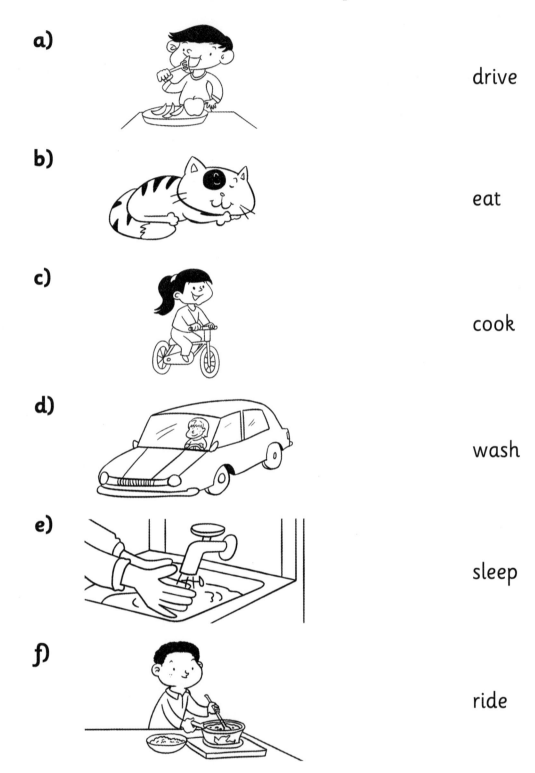

a)

b)

c)

d)

e)

f)

drive

eat

cook

wash

sleep

ride

2 **Look at the pictures. Listen and circle the activities you can see. Say or write them.**

a)

b)

_____

c)

d)

_____

e)

f)

_____

3 Complete the sentences. Choose words from the box.

| can   can't   can   is |

a)

Gran _____ asleep on the bed.

b)

She _____ ride a bike.

c)

He _____ cook supper.

d)

The baby _____ wash his face.

4 Complete these sentences about things you can and can't do.

a) I can _____.

b) I can't _____.

5 **Listen to the sentences. Circle all the words with the same 'a' sound as in** *cat***.**

a) I have got a cat and a hat.

b) My gran has a nap in the afternoon.

c) I've got an apple in my hand.

d) Can you ride a bike? I can!

6 **Complete the words.**

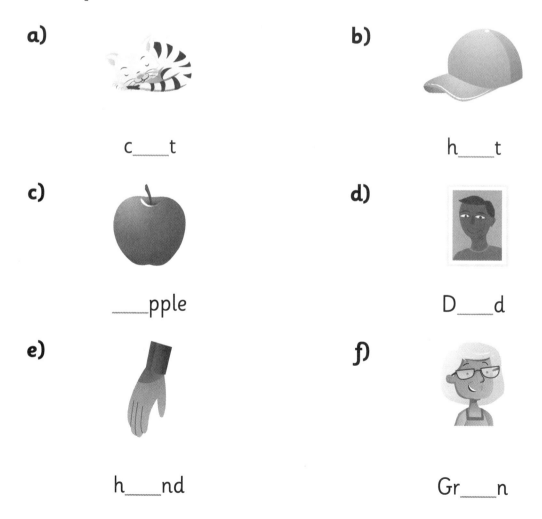

a)

c____t

b)

h____t

c)

____pple

d)

D____d

e)

h____nd

f)

Gr____n

7 **Read the story _Dad, Gran and the Cat Take a Nap_ in the Student's Resource Book. Complete the sentences with a word from the box.**

cat   Dad   Gran   nap

a)

_____ needs a nap.

b)

_____ is on the chair.

c)

The _____ is on the bench.

d)

Dad has a _____.

8 **Write the correct word from the box under each picture.**

| brush   cook   eat   hop   play   ride   run   sleep   wash |

a)

_____

b)

_____

c)

_____

d)

_____

e)

_____

f)

_____

g)

_____

h)

_____

i)

_____

Unit 2 Progress check

1 Listen and tick ✓ the words.

a)

he	it	she
she	that	he

b)

mother	grandpa	uncle
father	grandma	aunty

2 Listen and tick ✓ the pictures.

a)

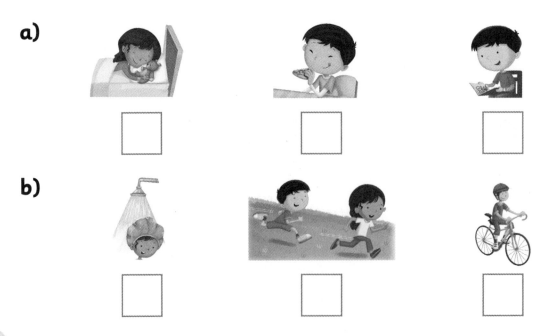

b)

3 Complete the words.

a)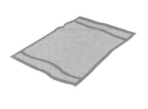

m___t

b)

h___nd

4 Circle the correct word.

a)

eat   sleep

b)

cook   book

c)

bike   bag

d)

wash   dish

Unit 3 Our colourful world

Week 1 Colours

1 Listen and draw.

2 **Listen and colour in the picture.**

3 **Write the names of some colours in your picture.**

_____

4 Look at the pictures. Say the words. Write the beginning sounds.

a)

 _____C_____

b)

 _____

c)

 _____

d)

 _____

e)

 _____

f)

 _____

g)

 _____

h)

 _____

5 **Colour in the colour words in the puzzle using the correct colour.**

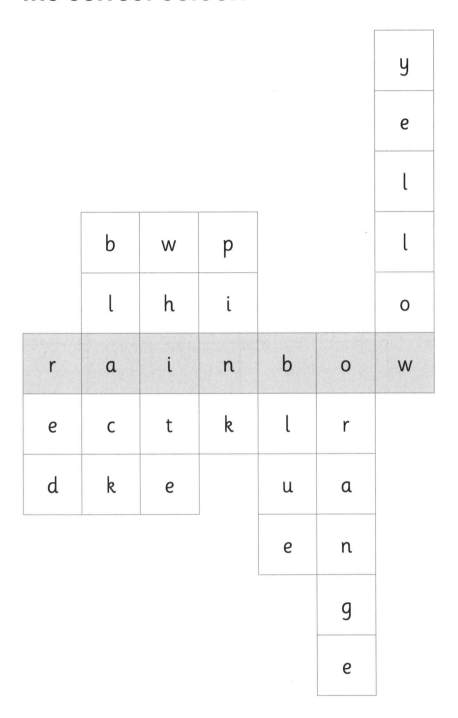

Read the word in the grey blocks.

6 **Use a different colour to colour in these things. Write the name of the colour you use.**

A _____ notebook.

A _____ book.

A _____ pencil.

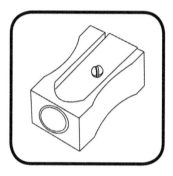

A _____ sharpener.

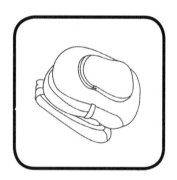

A _____ bag.

A _____ ruler.

7 **Choose four different things you can see in the classroom. Draw them and count how many you can see.**

	Draw	How many?
1		
2		
3		
4		

Week 2 Describing things

1 **Listen to the story *Rat-a-tat-tat*. Colour in the picture.**

2 **Use the words from the box to label the picture.**

| blue | cat | fox | hat | socks | white | yellow |

3 **Listen to the sentences. Circle all the words with the same 'o' sound, as in _fox_.**

a) The   dog   and   the   frog   are   in   the   box.

b) The   book   is   on   the   table.

4 **Listen to the sentences. Circle all the words with the same 'a' sound, as in _cat_.**

a) The   bad   bat   makes   the   mouse   sad.

b) The   bat   makes   the   owl   mad.

5 **Complete the words.**

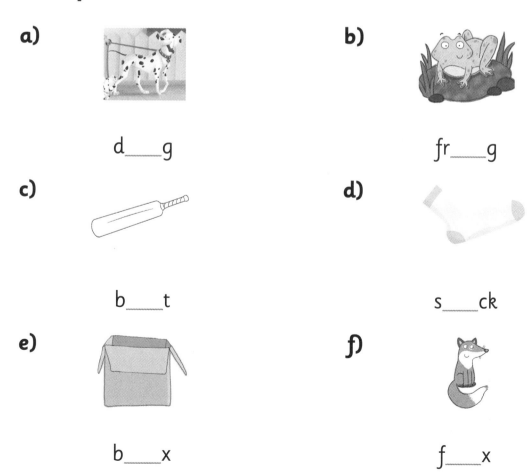

a)

d____g

b)

fr____g

c)

b____t

d)

s____ck

e)

b____x

f)

f____x

6 **Choose the correct sentences from the box.**

Copy the sentences next to the pictures.

| Bat tricks Fox. | Owl is mad. |
| Bat tricks Mouse. | The dog is big. |

a)

_____

_____

b)

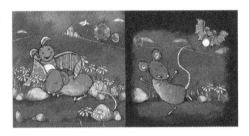

_____

_____

c)

_____

_____

d)

_____

_____

7 **Look at the pictures. What shapes can you see?**

8 **Count the shapes you can see in the pictures.**
Write your answers.

a) squares   **b)** circles   **c)** rectangles

_____   _____   _____

d) triangles   **e)** stars   **f)** hexagons

_____   _____   _____

Week 3 How many?

1 **Draw lines to match the numbers and the words.**

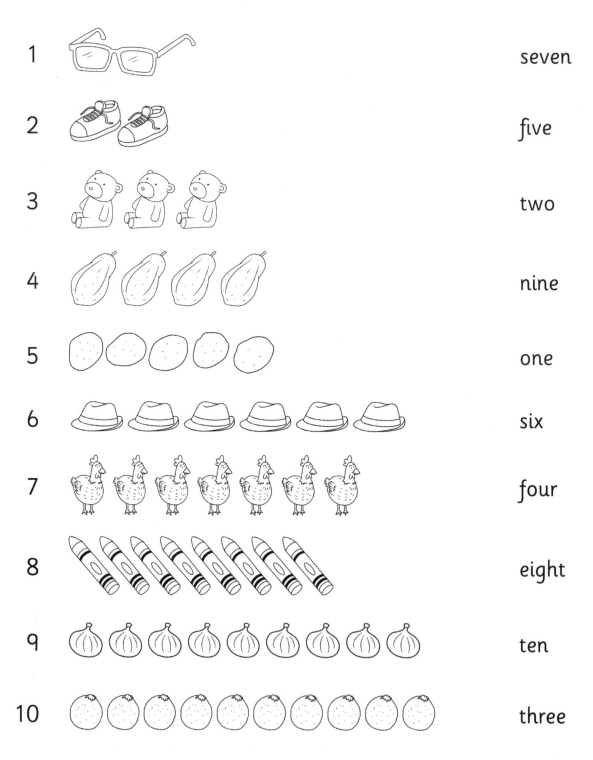

1	seven
2	five
3	two
4	nine
5	one
6	six
7	four
8	eight
9	ten
10	three

2 **Circle the correct words.**

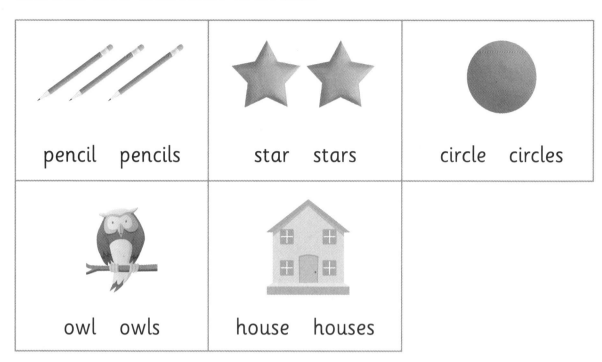

pencil   pencils

star   stars

circle   circles

owl   owls

house   houses

3 **Tick ✓ the correct sentences.**

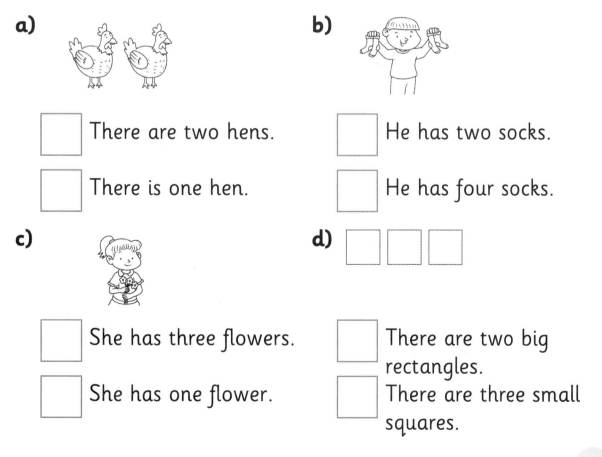

a)

☐ There are two hens.

☐ There is one hen.

b)

☐ He has two socks.

☐ He has four socks.

c)

☐ She has three flowers.

☐ She has one flower.

d)

☐ There are two big rectangles.

☐ There are three small squares.

4 Complete the game. Fill in the numbers.

- Play the game in pairs.
- Spin a spinner.
- Move your counters.
- Say the numbers.

Unit 3 **Progress check**

1 Listen and tick ✓ the words.

☐ yellow   ☐ white

☐ red   ☐ pink

☐ blue   ☐ brown

☐ orange   ☐ grey

☐ green   ☐ purple

☐ black

2 Complete the words.

a)

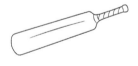

b _____ t

b)

_____ _____ x

c)

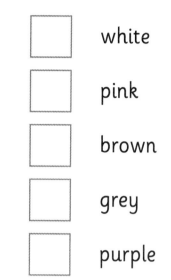

_____ _____ x

d)

_____ _____ g

3 Choose the correct word. Write the word under the picture.

> circle   eight   mouse   owl   rainbow
> six   square   triangle   two

a)

_____

b)

_____

c)

_____

d)

_____

e)

_____

f)

_____

g)

_____

h)

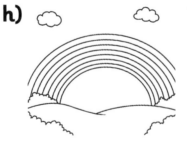

_____

i)

_____

Unit 4 Food

Week 1 Fruit and vegetables

1 **Write the first letter of each word. Then draw your own picture.**

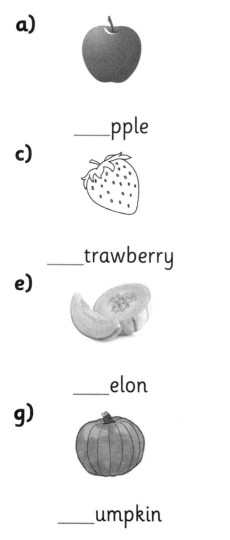

a)

____pple

b)

____range

c)

____trawberry

d)

____rapes

e)

____elon

f)

____ango

g)

____umpkin

h)

____arrot

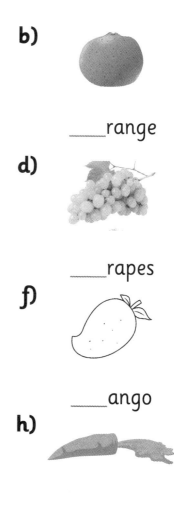

2 **How many are there? Write the number words, then complete the words.**

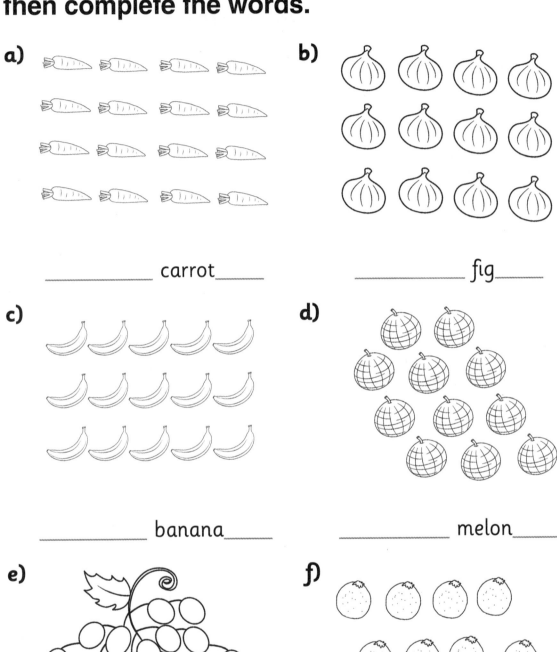

a)

_____ carrot_____

b)

_____ fig_____

c)

_____ banana_____

d)

_____ melon_____

e)

_____ grape_____

f)

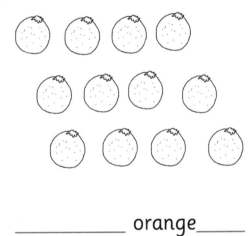

_____ orange_____

3 **Follow the instructions. Colour in the fruits.**
Circle the number words.

a) Colour in 11 apples.

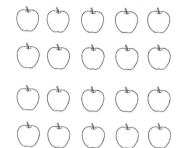

eleven   twelve

b) Colour in 16 star fruits.

seventeen   sixteen

c) Colour in 14 mangoes.

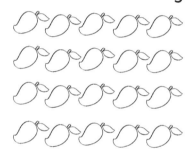

seventeen   fourteen

d) Colour in 15 bananas.

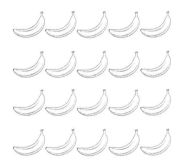

fifteen   fourteen

e) Colour in 20 plums.

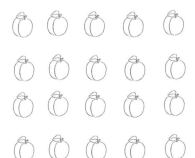

twelve   twenty

f) Colour in 13 pineapples.

fourteen   thirteen

4 **Find the fruit and vegetable words in the word search puzzle.**

apple	bean	cabbage	grape	guava
mango	onion	peach	potato	spinach

a	p	p	l	e	c	p	b	s
h	g	m	o	p	a	z	v	p
g	r	a	p	e	b	x	n	i
u	k	n	q	a	b	e	a	n
a	i	g	r	c	a	o	e	a
v	j	o	s	h	g	n	y	c
a	k	t	y	u	e	i	o	h
m	p	o	t	a	t	o	f	m
l	g	b	u	w	c	n	s	i

5 Read the riddles. Draw pictures to show the answers.

a) I am long. I am orange and I am crunchy to eat. What am I?

b) I am small and round. I am green or red or yellow. I am soft and sweet. What am I?

c) I am big and round. I am orange or yellow. You cook me. What am I?

Week 2 Let's eat

1 Complete the words under each picture.

a)

_____ake

b)

_____gg

c)

_____oghurt

d)

_____izza

e)

_____andwich

f)

_____ea

g)

_____ater

h)

_____pple

i)

ch___c___late

2 Find the names of six vegetables in the puzzle.

carrotbeanpumpkinonionpotatospinach

3 Tick ✓ the correct sentence under each picture.

a)

☐ The ants like cake.

☐ The ants don't like cake.

b)

☐ The ants like apple.

☐ The ants don't like apple.

c)

☐ The ants like chocolate.

☐ The ants don't like chocolate.

d)

☐ Dad is sleeping.

☐ Dad is eating.

4 What are they doing? Circle the correct word.

a)

drinking   playing

b)

drawing   reading

c)

playing   eating

d)

jumping   playing

e)

writing   drinking

f)

singing   sleeping

5 **Draw things you need to make pancakes.**
Write the word underneath your picture.

eggs   flour   milk   sugar

6 Match the words and the times.

breakfast   tea   snack

dinner   lunch

7 What time do you have breakfast? Draw the hands on the clock.

Week 3 What I like

1 **Read *What do you like?* again. Answer the questions. Tick ✓ the answers.**

a) What does she like for breakfast?

☐ eggs

☐ porridge

☐ toast

b) What does he like for a snack?

☐ yoghurt

☐ an apple

☐ cake

c) What does he like for lunch?

☐ a sandwich

☐ pizza

☐ baked potato

2 **Circle the correct words.**

a)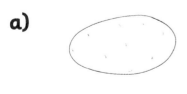

potato   sandwich

b)

cake   cereal

c)

biscuit   banana

3 Answer the questions. Draw pictures.
Describe your pictures to your group.

a) What do you like for breakfast?

I like _____ and _____ .

b) What do you like for a snack?

I like _____ .

c) What do you like for dinner?

I _____ .

4 Look at the graph. Answer the questions.

What we like to drink

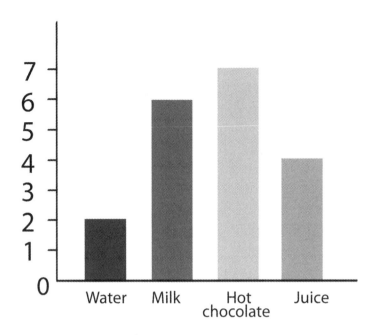

a) How many children like water?

_____

b) How many children like juice?

_____

c) What do most children like?

_____

d) How many children answered the questions?

_____

5 Listen to the questions. Write Yes or No.

a) Do you like swimming? _____

b) Do you like yoghurt? _____

c) Do you like reading? _____

d) Do you like toast and tea? _____

e) Do you like sandwiches? _____

f) Do you like cereal with milk for breakfast? _____

6 Complete the sentences.

a) I like _____ and _____.

b) I don't like _____ and _____.

Unit 4 Progress check

1 Complete the words.

a)

10

t____n

b)

____range

c)

____ ____s

d)

____ean

e)

____ ____n

f)

____ineapple

2 Count and write the numbers.

a)

There are _____ mangoes.

b)

There are _____ strawberries.

3 **Look at the pictures. Circle the correct word.**

a)

lunch   breakfast

b)

reading   eating

4 **What do you like to eat? Draw a picture.**
Write two sentences.

This is _____.

I like _____.

Unit 5 Let's have fun

Week 1 Fun and games

1 Look at the pictures. Listen and tick ✓ the boxes.

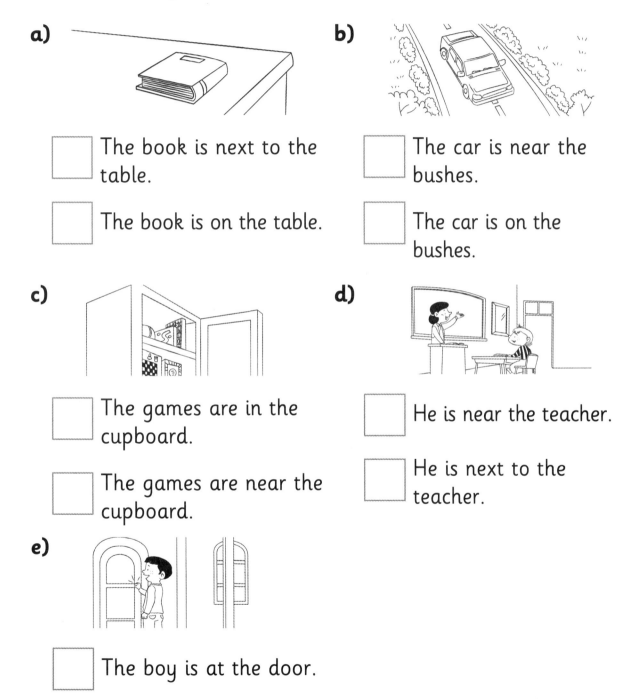

a)

☐ The book is next to the table.

☐ The book is on the table.

b)

☐ The car is near the bushes.

☐ The car is on the bushes.

c)

☐ The games are in the cupboard.

☐ The games are near the cupboard.

d)

☐ He is near the teacher.

☐ He is next to the teacher.

e)

☐ The boy is at the door.

☐ The boy is in the door.

2 Where is the boy? Underline the correct words under each picture.

a)

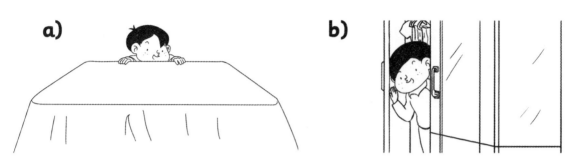

behind the table   under the table

b)

in the cupboard   on the cupboard

c)

behind the door   on the door

d)

in the bed   under the bed

3 Read the sentences. Draw the pictures.

The girl is next to a sofa.

A boy is near a fridge.

4 Make sentences with these words.

a) on is She bike her

_____

_____.

b) near door the is He

_____

_____.

c) me plays sister with My

_____

_____.

d) games like I

_____

_____.

e) ball with We play a

_____

_____.

5 Listen to the instructions. Play the snakes and ladders game.

- Write the missing numbers.
- Draw three snakes.
- Draw three ladders.
- Play the game in groups.

50	49	48	47	46	45	44	43	42	41
31	32	33	34	35		37	38		40
30	29	28	27	26	25	24	23	22	21
11									
	9					4			1

Start

6 **Look at the words in the box. Find and circle the words in the sentences.**

> is   my   on   the   this   under   up   we

a) The cat is under the table.

b) The book is on the desk.

c) These are my socks.

d) This is my hat.

e) We are going up the tree.

7 **Write four new sentences. Use a word from the box in each sentence.**

a) _____.

b) _____.

c) _____.

d) _____.

Week 2 We like doing sports

1 **Match the words and the pictures. Write the word under the picture.**

> athletics   netball   cycling   swimming
> football   tennis   hockey   judo

a)

_____

b)

_____

c)

_____

d)

_____

e)

_____

f)

_____

g)

_____

h)

_____

2 Listen to the instructions. Complete the picture.

- Draw the ball.
- Draw the goal.
- Draw a whistle.
- Colour in the T-shirts to show the two teams.

3 Look at the graph. Listen and answer the questions.

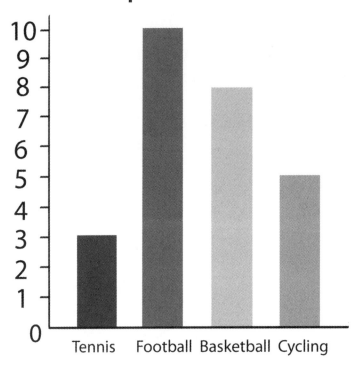

The sports that we like

a) How many children like playing tennis?

_____

b) How many children like cycling?

_____

c) What do most children like doing?

_____

d) How many children answered the questions?

_____

4 Make sentences with these words.

a) are There teams two

_____

_____ .

b) whistle The referee got a has

_____

_____ .

c) sea in the Peter Ali swimming like and

_____

_____ .

5 Copy these sentences. Add capital letters.

a) i play football at the club

_____

_____ .

b) there are two goals on the field

_____

_____ .

c) chris likes cycling

_____

_____ .

6 **Complete the sentences. Choose the best word.**

a) There _____ two goals on the football field. (is/are)

b) She _____ playing volleyball. (like/likes)

c) Let's _____ a computer game. (play/playing)

7 **Draw a picture of a sport that you like playing. Write a sentence about it.**

Week 3 The race

1 Listen and follow the instructions.

a) Circle the 1st box.

b) Colour the 3rd box yellow.

c) Colour the 4th box red.

d) Colour the 10th box blue.

e) Draw a pen in the 5th box.

f) Draw a ball in the 7th box.

1st ☐

2nd ☐

3rd ☐

4th ☐

5th ☐

6th ☐

7th ☐

8th ☐

9th ☐

10th ☐

2 Look at the pictures. Draw the hands on the clocks. Underline the correct words.

a)

in the morning
in the afternoon

b)

in the morning
in the evening

c)

in the afternoon
in the evening

d)

in the evening
in the morning

3 Find the names of five days of the week in the puzzle. Write the words in the correct order.

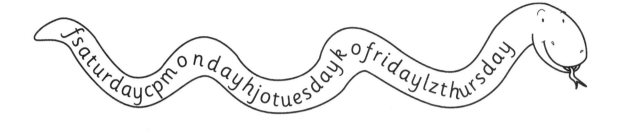

....

....

....

....

....

4 Circle the correct words to complete the sentences.

a) We go to school (at/on) seven o'clock.

b) My mum makes supper (in/on) the evening.

c) My family have lunch together (at/on) Sundays.

d) We do not go to school (on/at) Saturdays.

e) I like running (at/in) the mornings.

f) My sister goes to bed (in/at) eight o'clock.

Unit 5 Progress check

1 **Listen and tick ✓ the pictures that your teacher describes.**

a)

b)

c)

6th 7th 3rd

2 Complete the sentences.

a)

He is _____ (at/on) the door.

b)

The book is next _____ (on/to) the chair.

c)

The cat is _____ (in/on) the lamp.

d)

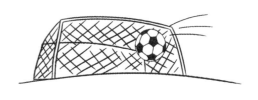

The ball is _____ (in/behind) the net.

3 Complete the words. Write the first letters.

a) _____ycling

b) _____ootball

c) _____ockey

d) _____udo

e) _____etball

f) _____olleyball

g) _____ _____estling

h) _____ _____imming

Unit 6 Out and about

What can I wear?

1 **Tick ✓ the correct word to match the names of the clothes.**

a)
- [ ] jacket
- [ ] jeans

b)
- [ ] skirt
- [ ] shorts

c)
- [ ] skirt
- [ ] scarf

d)
- [ ] sunglasses
- [ ] sandals

e)
- [ ] shorts
- [ ] T-shirt

f)
- [ ] glasses
- [ ] shoes

g)
- [ ] dress
- [ ] blouse

h)
- [ ] jumper
- [ ] trousers

i)
- [ ] gloves
- [ ] jacket

j)
- [ ] sock
- [ ] coat

2 Complete the words.

a)

_____ _____ess

b)

_____ _____oes

c)

_____ _____asses

d)

_____ _____irt

e)

_____ _____ousers

f)

_____ _____arf

g)

_____ _____oves

h)

_____ _____orts

3 **Look at the pictures and read the clues.**
Complete the words. The first one has been
done for you.

1	s	h	o	e	s
2					
3					
4					
5					

Clues

1 You wear two of these.

2 This word begins with *sk*.

3 Girls and boys wear these.

4 You can wear this when it is cold.

5 You wear these on your feet.

4 **Listen to the story *Where Are My Jeans?* Complete the sentences. Use words from the box.**

bed	dress	on	one	under

a) The jeans are _____ the bed.

b) The scarf is _____ the chair

c) The _____ is in the cupboard.

d) The T-shirt and jacket are on the _____.

e) There is _____ sock under the bed.

5 **Draw these clothes on the washing line.**

shorts   four socks   two T-shirts   a dress

6 Listen to the poems. Then say them.

1. Here are Grandpa's glasses
And here is Grandpa's hat
And there's the way he folds his arms
And takes a little nap.

2. One potato, two potatoes,
three potatoes, four!
Five potatoes, six potatoes,
Seven potatoes – and more!

3. I like paw-paws
And I like plums
I like painting
But I don't like drums.

4. Red, red, red,
    Touch your head.
Blue, blue, blue,
    Touch your shoe.
Black, black, black,
    Hands behind your back.
Green, green, green,
    Shout and scream!

7 Complete the sentences. Use words from the box.

is	not	She	putting

a) This is my Grandma. _____ wears glasses.

b) That _____ my sister. She likes wearing dresses.

c) I do _____ like wearing a hat.

d) He is _____ on his clothes.

8 Use these words to make sentences.

a) She her shoes taking off is

_____.

b) I my socks putting on am

_____.

c) likes He wearing shorts

_____.

d) They wearing are gloves

_____.

Week 2 At the weekend

1 Read the poem and circle these words.

a	and	ball	down	I'm	me	on	the	up

The Ball Song

Throw me up and catch me,
bounce me on the ground,
put me down and twist me,
twizzle me around.

Drop me on the floor,
kick me at the wall.
Bounce me! Bounce me!
I'm a bouncy ball.

2 Find words in the poem that begin with the same letters.

b _____

a _____

tw _____

th _____

d _____

3 **Read the story _Super Ben_. Then complete the sentences. Use words from the box.**

plays	draws	feeds	splashes

a) Ben _____ a picture.

b) He _____ the ducks.

c) He _____ on the roundabout.

d) He _____ in the puddles.

4 **Where does Ben go? Underline the correct answers.**

to the park   to school

on the roundabout   in the picture

5 **Read the sentence. Draw the picture.**

There are three brown ducks in a puddle.

6 Look at the pictures. Write a verb from the box in the first gap in the sentences.

play	cleans	eat	visit

a)

They _____ games _____.

b)

He _____ his bedroom _____.

c)

They _____ lunch together _____.

d)

They _____ friends _____.

7 Now choose a time from the box to complete the sentences above.

at the weekend   after school   on Sundays   in the afternoon

8 **Draw lines to match the words with the same end sounds.**

hat	lap
wall	three
me	play
day	cat
nap	ball

9 **Write adjectives from the box with the same beginning sound.**

Example:

> a **busy** bee

bouncy	busy	green	pretty

a) a _____ bee

b) _____ grass

c) a _____ ball

d) a _____ picture

Week 3 How I feel

1 Describe the weather. Choose a word from the box to complete each sentence.

cloudy	rainy	sunny	windy

a)

It is a _____ day.

b)

It is a _____ day.

c)

It is a _____ day.

d)

It is a _____ day.

2 How does the weather make you feel?
Tick ✓ a box.

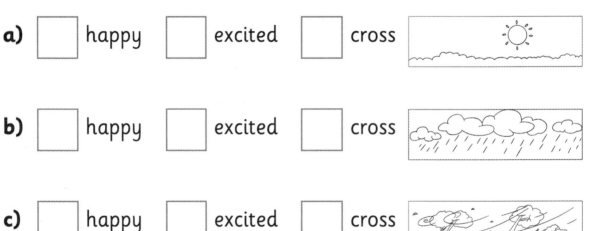

a) ☐ happy ☐ excited ☐ cross

b) ☐ happy ☐ excited ☐ cross

c) ☐ happy ☐ excited ☐ cross

3 Copy the correct sentence under each picture.

Bob is sad and lonely.　　　He opens the door.

Bob tells his friends to go.　　Bob is happy again.

Bob has a treehouse.　　　His friends are noisy.

a)

_____

b)

_____

c)

_____

d)

_____

e)

_____

f)

_____

4 Listen to the instructions. Work in groups and play *The Weather Game*.

- Take turns.
- Spin a spinner.
- Read the instructions.
- Play the game.

8	9	10 Go back to NINE.	FINISH
7 Go on to EIGHT	6	5 Go back to TWO.	4 Go on to SIX.
START	1 Go on to TWO.	2	3 Miss a turn.

5 Read the sentences. Draw pictures to match.

I feel sad.   I feel happy.

6 Make two sentences with each group of words.

a) raining it is I happy am

_____

_____.

b) cold wet and it is cross am I

_____

_____.

7 Look at the pictures. Say the words. Which words have the same middle sounds as *pail*? Tick ✓ the pictures.

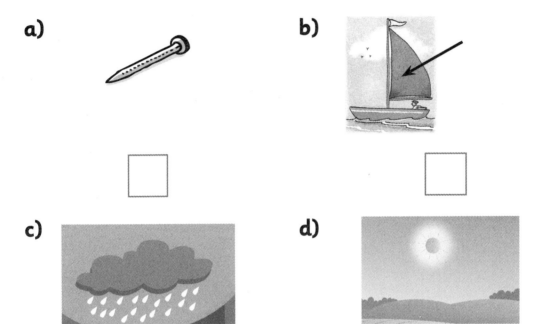

a)

b)

c)

d)

8 Complete the names of days of the week.

Mond ____ ____

Sund ____ ____

Thursd ____ ____

9 Complete these words with *-ee*.

tr ____ ____

ʃ ____ ____ l

Unit 6 Progress check

1 Write the correct word under each picture.

> boots   glasses   sandals   shorts   sweatshirt
>
> coat   jeans   T-shirt   sock

_____   _____   _____

_____   _____   _____

_____   _____   _____

2 Make sentences with each group of words.

a) sunny It is

_____ .

b) cross am I

_____ .

c) We games play Saturdays on

_____ .

3 Complete the sentences. Choose words from the box.

| play | draws | feeds | splash |

a) I _____ in the puddles.

b) He _____ the ducks.

c) They _____ on the roundabout.

d) She _____ pictures.

Unit 7 Our world

Week 1 Homes

1 **Label the outside parts of the house. Use the words in the box. Find the words in the Student's Resource Book on page 44.**

door	garage	garden	gate	roof	window

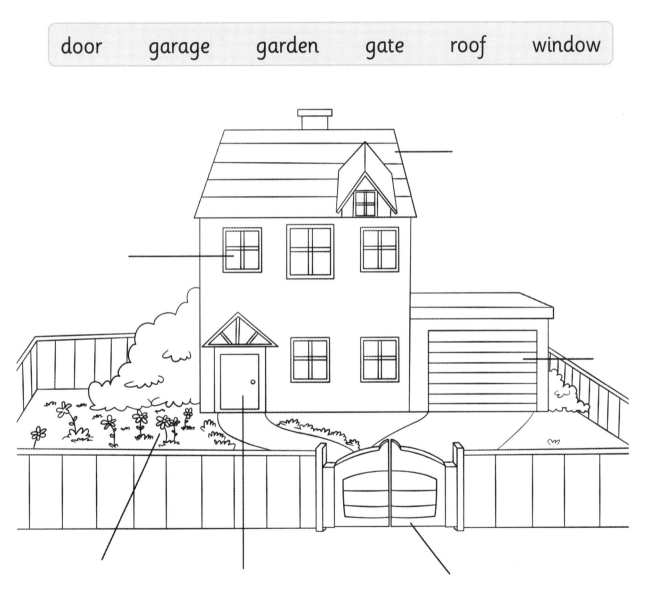

2 Label the furniture in the kitchen. Use the words from the box.

chair   cooker   cupboard   fridge   sink

table   tap   washing machine

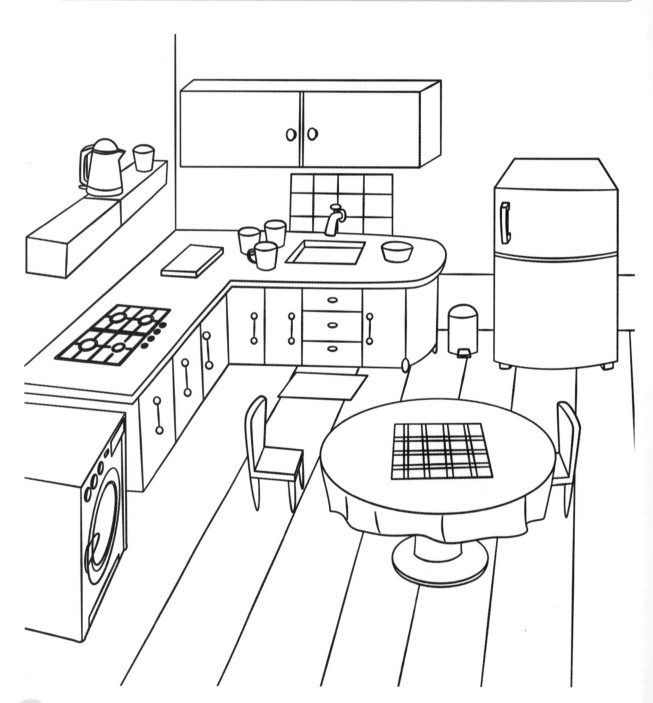

3 **Look at the pictures. Complete each sentence with the best word from the box.**

| wheels | quiet | water | noisy |

This home is _____.   This home is on _____.

4 **Draw a picture of your own home. Write a sentence to describe it. Use some of the words from the box.**

| big | high | home | my | nice | noisy | quiet | small | warm |

5 **Listen to the story. Tick ✓ the sentence that matches each picture.**

a)

| | This is my new home. |
| | This is our new boat. |

b)

| | My new bed is big! |
| | My new home is noisy. |

c)

| | I am happy. |
| | I am sad. |

d)

| | I haven't got a friend. I am sad. |
| | This is my new friend. I am happy. |

6 **Find these words in the word search puzzle.**
Write the words.

a) One thing from a bedroom _____

_____

b) Two things from a bathroom _____

_____

c) Three things from a kitchen _____

_____

a	c	o	o	k	e	r	f
s	h	o	w	e	r	y	r
c	t	m	q	t	r	n	i
a	c	b	a	t	h	v	d
m	u	e	l	l	x	w	g
i	o	d	r	e	c	t	e

7 Listen to the instructions. Draw the house.

- Draw a rectangle.

- Draw a triangle on top of the house rectangle. This is the roof.

- Draw one door and three windows.

- Colour in the house.

8 **Read the sentences. Draw a picture for each sentence.**

This home is big.   This home is for a bird!

9 **Complete the sentences.**

Some homes are _____ up.

Some _____ are noisy.

Some homes _____ quiet.

Some homes float on _____.

Some homes _____ wheels.

10 Copy the sentences in the correct order.

I like playing football with Jo.

We are moving to a new home.

One day I make a new friend, Jo.

My new home is small but it has a big garden.

_____

_____

_____

_____

_____

_____

_____

11 Tell the story to your partner.

Week 2 Plants and animals

1 **Draw a picture of a plant. Colour in your picture. Label the following parts:**

> leaf   roots   stem

2 **Complete the sentences. Choose the correct word.**

a) Plants grow from _____. (seeds/goats)

b) Plants need soil, _____ and water to grow. (sun/fun)

3 **Look at the diagram. Listen to the text.**

The life cycle of a bean plant

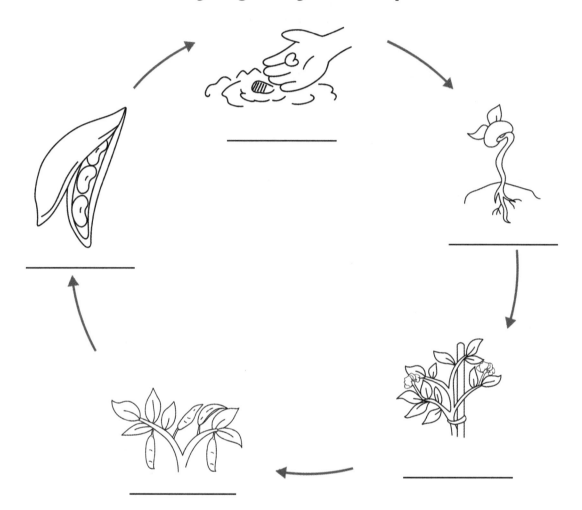

_____

_____

_____

_____

_____

4 **Copy the correct sentence under each picture.**

There are seeds inside the pod.

We plant the seed in the ground.

The seed grows.

The plant has flowers.

There are beans on the plant.

5 Listen to the story *The Very Big Carrot*. Who helps to pull up the carrot? Label the pictures.

| Mrs Brown | Mr Brown | boy | girl | cat | goat | horse |

a)

_____

b)

_____

c)

_____

d)

_____

e)

_____

f)

_____

g)

_____

6 Read the story of *Jack and the Beanstalk.* Circle these words in the story:

an	and	are	his	is	the

Jack and his mother are poor.

Jack gives the cow to an old man.

Jack gets some beans.

Jack's mother is cross.

The beans grow.

Jack meets the giant.

Jack finds gold.

Jack's mother is happy.

7 Answer the questions. Circle the correct answer.

a) What does Jack sell?   cow   giant

b) What does Jack get?   beans   flowers

c) What do the beans do?   grow   plant

d) What does Jack find?   gold   green

8 **Read these sentences from the story *The Very Big Carrot*.**

The goat helps.

The girl helps.

The cat helps.

Mrs Brown pulls up the carrots.

The horse helps.

They all fall over!

Mr Brown helps.

The boy helps.

9 **Listen to the story. Copy the sentences in the correct order.**

Week 3 Living in our world

1 **Read the story *The Oak Tree* in the Student's Resource Book. Find words in the story to label this picture of an oak tree.**

a)
_____

b)
_____

c)
_____

d)
_____

e) _____

2 **Find the names of these animals in the story.**

a)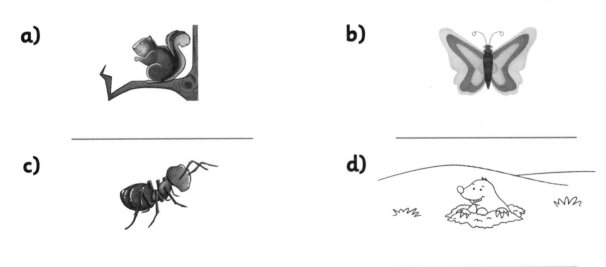

b)

c)

d)

_____

3 Label the things in the picture with words from the box.

butterfly	crow	bat	wasp	mole
squirrel	owl	caterpillar	ant	worm
fox	beetle	woodpecker	rabbit	

a)

b)

c)

d)

e)

_____ _____ _____ _____ _____

f)

g)

h)

i)

j)

_____ _____ _____ _____ _____

k)

l)

m)

n)

_____ _____ _____ _____

4 Read the story *The Oak Tree* again. Complete the sentences using the words from the box.

the	are	has	in	is	and

a) A tree _____ branches _____ a trunk.

b) There _____ bark on _____ trunk.

c) Crows and bats live _____ the branches.

d) These _____ the roots of the tree.

5 Find the names of six animals that live in an oak tree in the word search. Look on page 48 in your Student's Resource Book.

x	b	q	z	c	k	b	y	w
s	q	u	i	r	r	e	l	a
y	k	p	b	o	e	e	z	s
j	d	x	p	w	t	t	j	p
x	h	b	e	e	t	l	e	x
q	z	a	a	y	b	e	b	q
b	u	t	t	e	r	f	l	y

6 Write the correct words under the photographs.

a)

_____

b)

_____

c)

_____

d)

_____

| desert | mountains | jungle | South Pole |

7 Complete the sentences with words from the box.

| dry | hot | wet | cold |

a) It is _____ at the South Pole.

b) A desert is _____ .

c) It is _____ and _____ in a jungle.

8 Look at the map. Label the map with these names.

| Africa | North America | Asia |
| South America | Europe | Oceania |

Our world

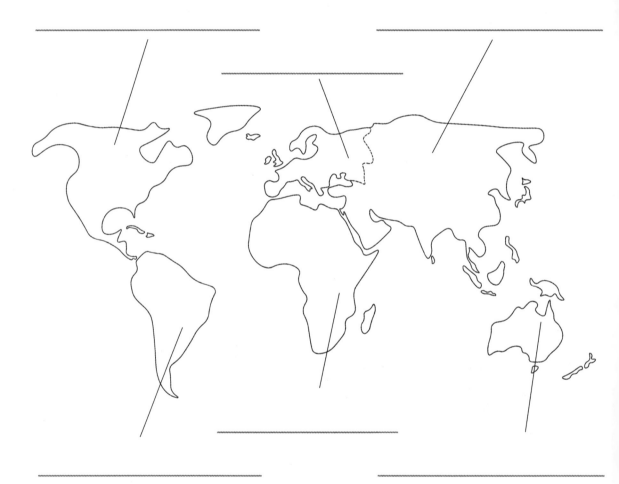

9 Draw a picture of one of these places:

- a jungle
- a mountain
- a very cold place
- a very hot place

10 Complete the sentences about your picture.

This is a _____.

It is _____ and

_____.

_____

_____ live here.

Unit 7 Progress check

1 Listen and underline the word that you hear.

a) door floor

b) gate Kate

c) fridge dish

d) bin pin

e) Tuesday Thursday

f) wheel meal

2 Circle the word that matches each picture.

a)

leaf   branch

b)

mouse   squirrel

c)

jungle   desert

d)

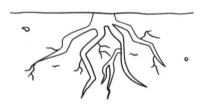

bark   roots

3 **Complete the sentences. Use words from the box.**

and	are	cold	in	is	two

a) There _____ lots of leaves on the tree.

b) My house has _____ bedrooms.

c) The kettle _____ in the kitchen.

d) It is very hot _____ dry in the desert.

e) The seeds grow _____ the bean pod.

f) The South Pole is _____ .

Unit 8 Healthy bodies

Week 1 My body

1 Use the words from the box to label the picture

arm   foot   hand   head   leg   neck   tummy

2 **The names of parts of the body are in the box. Find the words in the word search puzzle.**

arm	back	eyes	hand	head
leg	neck	nose	shoulder	toes

g	t	t	k	s	d	h	a
s	h	o	u	l	d	e	r
m	a	e	q	e	b	a	m
p	n	s	e	g	a	d	h
q	d	w	y	f	c	v	g
z	e	n	e	c	k	j	z
x	n	o	s	e	v	c	x
y	l	m	n	o	p	q	r

3 **Complete the sentences. Use words from the box.**

head   body   leg   back

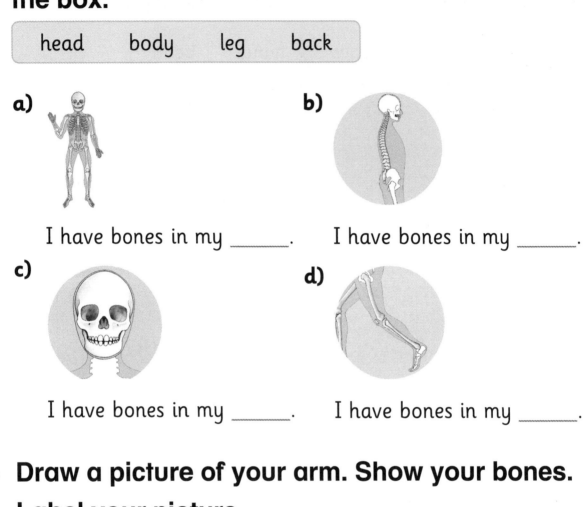

a)

I have bones in my _____.

b)

I have bones in my _____.

c)

I have bones in my _____.

d)

I have bones in my _____.

4 **Draw a picture of your arm. Show your bones. Label your picture.**

5 Make words. Add *-ing*.

a) paint ____ ____ ____

b) press ____ ____ ____

c) eat ____ ____ ____

d) wash ____ ____ ____

6 Look at the words on the board. Draw a picture about one of the words.

7 **Draw lines to match the parts of the body and the senses.**

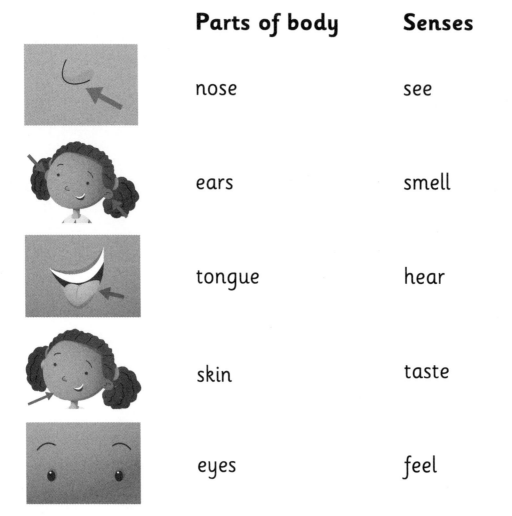

Parts of body	Senses
nose	see
ears	smell
tongue	hear
skin	taste
eyes	feel

8 **Complete the sentences.**

a) I see with my _____.

b) I taste with _____ _____.

c) I feel _____ _____ _____.

d) I _____ with my ears.

e) I _____ _____ _____ nose.

9 **Complete these poems about your hands and your senses. Give your poems titles.**

[title] _____

I use my hands

when I am _____

and when I am _____

and when I am _____ .

I use my hands all the time!

[title] _____

I hear with my _____

And I _____ with my

_____ .

I _____ with

my _____

And I _____ with my

_____ .

10 Draw pictures. Label your pictures.

Things I can hear	Things I can see

Things I can taste	Things I can smell

11 **Where do you have bones? Complete the list.**

You have bones in your _____ , your _____ ,

your _____ , your _____ , your _____

and your _____ .

12 **Draw a picture of your hands. Label your hands. Use these words:**

> left   hand   right   hand   finger   bone   nail

Week 2 Healthy and sick

1 **Read again about washing your hands on page 54 of the Student's Resource Book. Complete the instructions.**

1. Wet your _____ .

2. Put _____ on your hands.

3. _____ your hands together.

4. _____ to 20! Scrub your nails.

5. _____ off the soap.

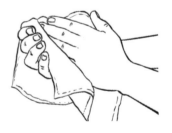

6. _____ your hands on a clean cloth.

2 **Complete the instructions. Use words and sentences from the box. The first one has been done for you.**

> toothbrush
>
> toothpaste
>
> a cup of water
>
> Rinse your mouth.
>
> Wet the toothbrush.
>
> Brush your teeth.
>
> Rinse your toothbrush.
>
> Put toothpaste on the toothbrush.

How to brush your teeth

You will need:

toothbrush

_____

_____

What you do:

1. _____

2. _____

3. _____

4. _____

5. _____

3 Think about how many glasses of water you drink every day. Write your estimate here.

_____ glasses

4 Keep a record for one week. Keep a tally here.

Days	Monday	Tuesday	Wednesday	Thursday	Friday
Number of glasses of water					
Total					

5 Complete the sentences.

I drink _____ glasses of water every day.

I drink _____ glasses of water every week.

6 Join the words to make sentences.

Put water and soap   your nails.

Then rub   the soap off your hands.

Scrub   to 20!

Count   your hands.

Rinse   on your hands.

Dry   your hands together.

7 Write the sentences here.

_____

_____

_____

_____

_____

8 **Match the sentences and the pictures.**

Write the sentences in the speech bubbles.

Take off your shoes.   Wet the soil.

Pick up the book.   Wash your hands.

a)

b)

c)

d)

Week 3 Oh no! I am sick!

1 **Look at the pictures. Write the illness from the box under the correct picture.**

> I have a headache.
>
> I have got a tummy ache.
>
> I have a sore throat.
>
> I have a cold.

a) _____

b) _____

c) _____

d) _____

2 **Read the story *In the Hospital* on page 55 of the Student's Resource Book. Complete the sentences with words from the box.**

| a | has | in | is |

a) Raj is _____ hospital.

b) The children make _____ card for Raj.

c) Raj _____ a sore leg.

d) He _____ feeling better.

3 **Make a card for Raj. Write a message and draw some pictures.**

Dear Raj
Get well soon.
From,
Ahmed

4 Draw lines to match the answers to the questions.

a) Do you feel sick?   No, I am not.

b) Is your head sore?   Yes, she does.

c) Are you well?   Yes, it is.

d) Does she have a cold?   Yes, they are.

e) Is he well?   Yes, I do.

f) Are they sick?   No, he isn't.

5 Complete the conversation.

Sam: Do _____ feel sick?

Anna: Yes, _____ do.

Sam: _____ you have a cold?

Anna: _____, I do.

Sam: Get better soon!

6 **Listen to the story *Sam the Big, Bad Cat* again. Complete the sentences.**

a)

_____ doesn't feel well.

b)

Sam is _____ the table.

c)

Sam is _____ the cupboard.

d)

Sam is _____ the shower.

e)

Tom doesn't _____ well.

f)

_____ feels better.

7 **Make sentences about the story with these words.**

a) Tom has cat bad big a

_____.

b) Sam not does well feel

_____.

c) to the vet We're going

_____.

d) Sam in the cupboard hides

_____.

e) in the shower Sam hides

_____.

f) Tom Sam finds

_____.

g) Tom not does well feel

_____.

Unit 8 Progress check

1 Listen and number the parts of the body.

2 **What do you need? Choose and write two words from the boxes.**

> soap   toothpaste   water

a) I need _____ and _____ to wash my hands.

> soap   toothpaste   water

b) I need _____ and _____ to brush my teeth.

3 **What is the first letter of each word? Circle the letter.**

a)

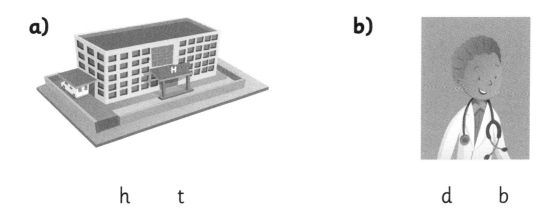

h   t

b)

d   b

4 **Make sentences from these groups of words.**

a) I well don't feel

_____.

b) He sick is

_____.

Week 1 My town

1 **Write the names of the places. Choose words from the box or add your own labels.**

doctor   library   park   school

shoe shop   swimming pool

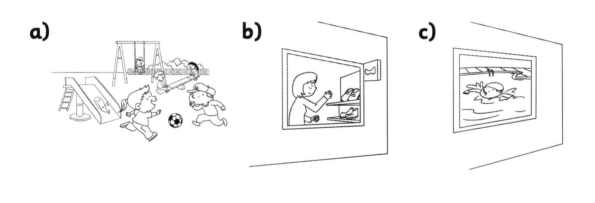

a)

b)

c)

_____   _____   _____

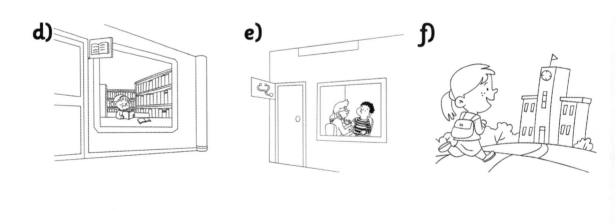

d)

e)

f)

_____   _____   _____

2 **Draw a picture of a place you like to visit.**

3 **Write two sentences about your picture.**

Start like this:

This is _____

_____ .

There _____

_____ .

4 Listen to the story *A Day Out* again.

- Follow on the map.
- Trace the path in colour.

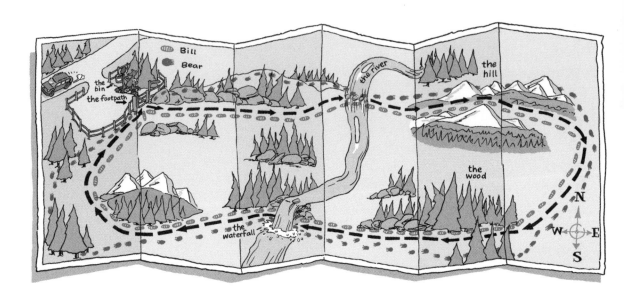

- Where do Bill and the bear go?
- Write the names of the places on the map here:

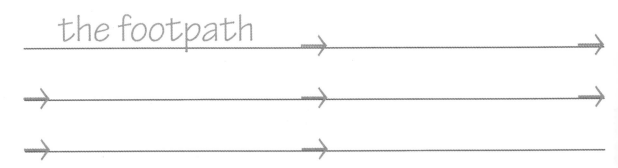

the footpath

5 Draw lines to match the words and the pictures.

a)

river

b)

hill

c)

wood

d)

waterfall

e)

litter bin

6 Choose the correct word to complete the sentences.

a) Bill goes _____ a walk. (for/to)

b) He goes _____ the hill. (up/into)

c) He goes _____ a river. (over/behind)

7 Imagine that you go out for the day.
Where do you go?

- Draw a map.
- Label the places on your map.
- Look in the box for some ideas!

pool   mountain   river   sea   dam   park   museum   beach

8 Write some sentences about one of the places on your map.

Start like this:

Here is _____

_____

_____.

Week 2 A day out

1 Draw lines to match the words and the pictures.

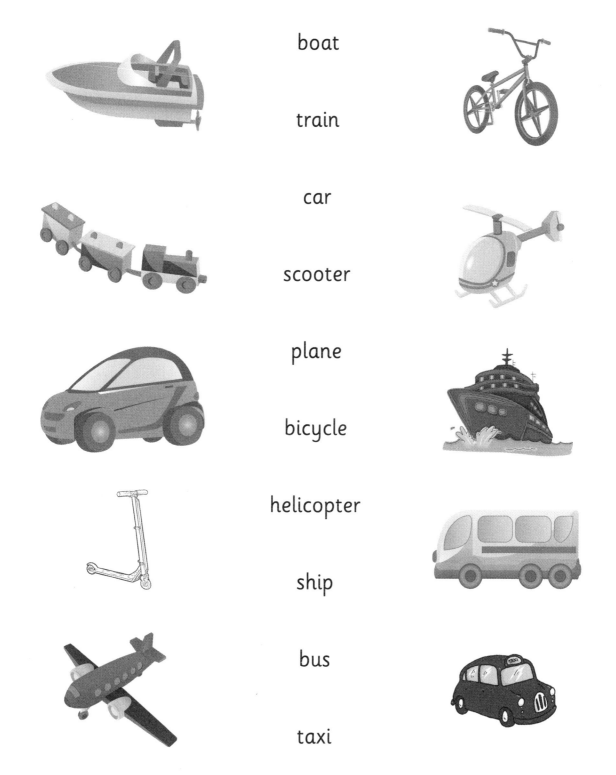

boat

train

car

scooter

plane

bicycle

helicopter

ship

bus

taxi

2 Colour in the pictures.

- The plane is red.
- The boat is green and blue.
- The taxi is red and black.

 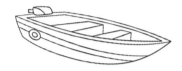 

3 Complete the pictures.

- The bike has two wheels.
- The bus has six wheels.

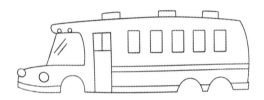

4 Draw a picture of a small boat and a big ship.

5 **Read the story *At the Bus Station* again.**

Tick ✓ the sentence that matches each picture.

a) ☐ They are packing suitcases.

☐ They are at the station.

b) ☐ They are playing at the station.

☐ They are at the station.

c) ☐ The girl is not there.

☐ The girl is there.

d) ☐ The girl is talking to a friend.

☐ The girl is packing a suitcase.

6 Look at the graph. Answer the questions.

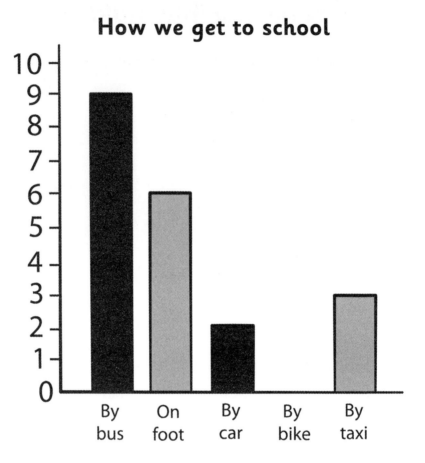

How we get to school

a) How many learners come by bus?

_____

b) How many learners walk?

_____

c) How do most learners get to school?

_____

d) Which type of transport do no learners use?

_____

7 Complete the chart.

One	More than one
train	trains
car	
taxi	
plane	
scooter	
bike	

8 Underline the correct words.

a) There (is/are) two cars in the park.

b) The taxi (is/are) next to the bus.

c) There are four (scooter/scooters) on the road.

d) Where is the (train/trains)?

9 **Find these words in the sentences.**
Circle the words.

are   don't   here   is   our   she   the   there   to   very   we

a) We   are   going   to   visit   our   cousins.

b) The   train   station   is   very   busy.

c) I   don't   know.   She   was   here.

d) Is   she   here?

e) There   you   are!

10 **Make questions with these groups of words.**
Use a capital letter to start each question.

a) he here is ?

_____

b) she is where ?

_____

c) you like trains do ?

_____

d) he does have a bike ?

_____

Week 3 Holidays

1 **Read the story *Around the World* on pages 62–63 of the Student's Resource Book again. Find the places on this map.**

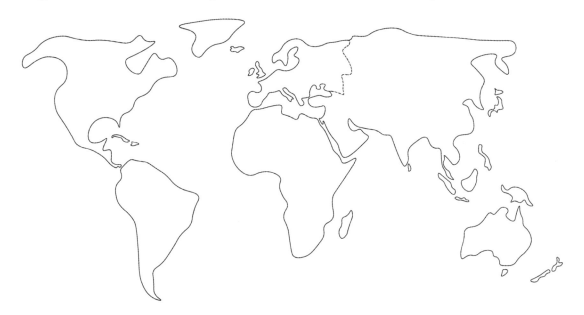

2 **Colour in these places in yellow on the map.**

- South America
- Africa
- India
- China

3 **Colour the other places in green. Colour the sea blue.**

4 **Draw a picture of something you think you can see in each place.**

5 **Underline three words to answer each question.**

a) Which countries do they visit?

India   China   Africa   America

b) How do they travel?

train   bike   plane   boat

c) What do they see?

bats   animals   houses   boats

6 **Where can you go? Write the names and how you can travel. Then write who you travel with.**

Name of place	How you travel	Who you travel with

7 Read the clues. Complete the puzzle. Most of the words are in the story *Around the World*.

Clues

1. The place where you live. My h____ ____ ____

2. A place where we all live. w____ ____ ____ ____

3. This flies up in the sky. p____ ____ ____ ____

4. A big country. C____ ____ ____ ____

5. Where _____ we go? d____ ____

6. This stops at a station. t____ ____ ____ ____

7. This word means talk or speak. s____ ____

8. This is yellow and round and up in the sky. s____ ____

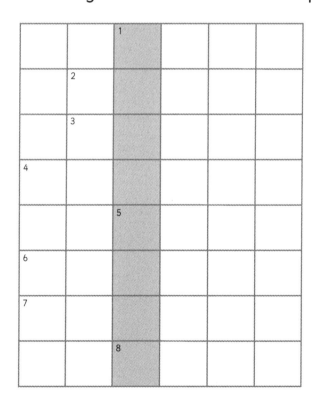

What new word can you see down the middle?

_____

8 Make sentences with words from each column.

  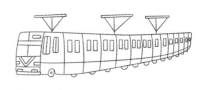

Let's go	on the train.
I like playing	you going?
We are	with my cousins.
She is going	they doing?
Where are	painting the house.
What are	to the park.

Write the sentences here.

a) _____

b) _____

c) _____

d) _____

e) _____

f) _____

The alphabet

Trace the letters. Draw a picture of something beginning with this letter.

Aa

Bb

Cc

Dd

Ee

Ff

Gg

Hh

Ii

Jj

Kk

Ll

Mm

Nn

Oo

Pp

Qq

Rr

Ss

Tt

Uu

Vv

Ww

Xx

Yy

Zz

Numbers

Trace the numbers and number words.

• 1 1 one	•• 2 2 two
••• 3 3 three	•••• 4 4 four
••••• 5 5 five	::: 6 6 six
:::: 7 7 seven	:::: 8 8 eight
::::: 9 9 nine	::::: 10 10 ten

11 11 eleven	12 12 twelve
13 13 thirteen	14 14 fourteen
15 15 fifteen	16 16 sixteen
17 17 seventeen	18 18 eighteen
19 19 nineteen	20 20 twenty

Trace the numbers and the words.

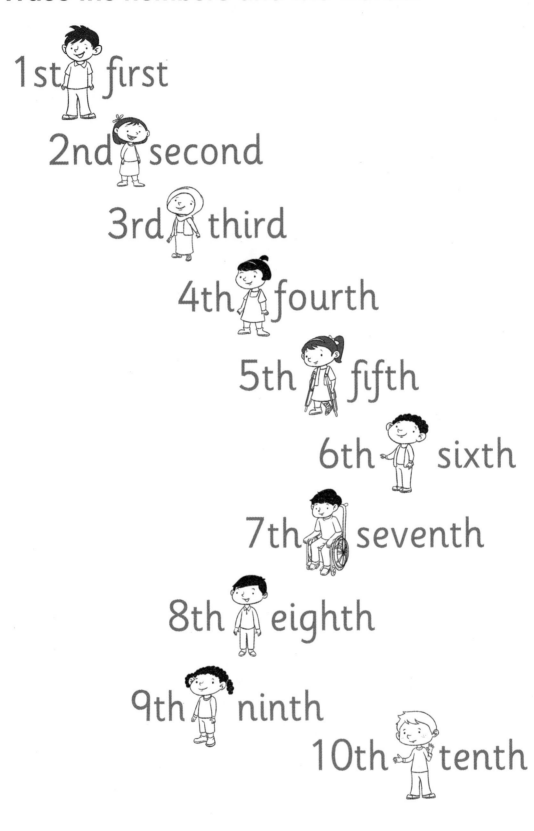

1st first

2nd second

3rd third

4th fourth

5th fifth

6th sixth

7th seventh

8th eighth

9th ninth

10th tenth